Comprehension Success

The Tiger

Tiger! Tiger!
burning bright

In the forests
of the night...

"Burning bright" is an example of alliteration.
What effect does this create?

Rachel Axten-Higgs

About this book

Ensuring children can read with good understanding is one of the main aims of the new primary curriculum. This book helps to improve comprehension skills across fiction, plays, poetry and non-fiction, breaking down each of these genres into easy-to-digest topics. Each topic is introduced by concise explanations and is explored through a variety of extract-based activities and questions. The test-style questions aid preparation for the **Reading paper** in the Key Stage 2 National Curriculum Tests (also known as SATs).

Features of the book

Key to comprehension provides concise explanations of the key concepts.

Comprehension material helps to explore each skill with an appropriate text, upon which *Practice activities* and *Test-style questions* are set.

Practice activities are designed to specifically help your child to understand the concept introduced in *Key to comprehension*.

Test-style questions help to build wider comprehension skills with questions reflecting those in the Key Stage 2 Reading National Curriculum Test.

Top tips give helpful hints to your child as they read and work through the topics.

Answers are in a pull-out booklet at the centre of the book.

Your child should keep referring to the extract while attempting the activities and questions. If they need more space to write an answer, encourage them to continue on a separate sheet of paper.

Comprehension tips

- Regular practice (10–15 minutes every day) will help your child to improve their reading. Take them to the library to let them discover different books and new authors. Reading a wide variety of books will keep it exciting and fun.
- Let your child read without distractions and only when they are relaxed and happy. Books can take them into new worlds and new experiences.
- Encourage your child to think about the text as they are reading. Does it make sense? If not, why not? It may be that they have misread a word and need to go back and correct themselves.
- Ask your child to read a particular page of a book and give them questions about it to test their understanding of the text.

When preparing for a reading test, remind your child to read the text **carefully**, read the question **carefully** and answer the question **using the text**. When asked, they should provide **evidence** from the text to back up their answer. Encourage them to **check** that they have fully answered the question.

Contents

Understanding complex texts

Key to comprehension

To develop as a reader, it is important to read different types of books by different authors from different times and places.

It can be fun to stick with a favourite author but this could mean that you do not learn to understand more complex texts. A good starting point is **classic fiction** – books written long ago that are still popular. Classic fiction reflects its own time, with different customs and the language of the time.

Comprehension material

Extract from *The Railway Children* by Edith Nesbit

But father did not seem to be able to get rid of the gentlemen at all quickly.

"I wish we HAD got a moat and a drawbridge," said Roberta; "then, when we didn't want people, we could just pull up the drawbridge and no one else could get in. I expect Father will have forgotten about when he was a boy if they stay much longer."

Mother tried to make the time pass by telling them a new fairy story about a Princess with green eyes, but it was difficult because they could hear the voices of Father and the gentlemen in the Library, and Father's voice sounded louder and different to the voice he generally used to people who came about testimonials and holiday funds.

Then the library bell rang, and everyone heaved a breath of relief.

"They're going now," said Phyllis; "he's rung to have them shown out."

But instead of showing anybody out, Ruth showed herself in, and she looked queer, the children thought.

"Please'm," she said, "the Master wants you to just step into the study. He looks like the dead, mam; I think he's had bad news. You'd best prepare yourself for the worst, 'm – p'raps it's a death in the family or a bank busted or – "

"That'll do, Ruth," said Mother gently; "you can go."

Then Mother went into the Library. There was more talking. Then the bell rang again, and Ruth fetched a cab. The children heard boots go out and down the steps. The cab drove away, and the front door shut. Then Mother came in. Her dear face was as white as her lace collar, and her eyes looked very big and shining. Her mouth looked like just a line of pale red – her lips were thin and not their proper shape at all.

Understanding complex texts

1. How would you describe Ruth? What does this tell you about the time period that the story is set in?

_____

_____

_____

2. From what Roberta says about her father forgetting, what might the family have been talking about before the visitors arrived?

_____

_____

_____

Test-style questions

1. What did Mother do to try to pass the time? Circle **one** answer.

Told a joke about a Princess with green eyes	Told a story about a Princess	Cooked the children some dinner	Listened to the voices in the Library

1 mark

2. Find and copy a simile used in the text and explain why the author has used it.

_____

_____

_____

2 marks

3. Why does Mother interrupt Ruth by telling her, "That'll do"?

_____

_____

1 mark

Words in context

Key to comprehension

In order to improve your comprehension of texts, you need to read widely and identify words that mean different things in different **contexts**. For example, older fiction uses language from the time it was written, whilst modern fiction uses modern vocabulary.

For example, **fabulous**:
- used to mean "related to fables"
- now means "wonderful", "superb" or "very good".

Even texts from the same era may use words that mean different things according to different contexts.

For example, **wicked**:
- can mean "evil"
- can mean "cool" or "excellent".

Top tip

Use the meaning of the whole sentence to help you understand the meaning of a word.

Comprehension material

Extract from *Treasure Island* by Robert Louis Stevenson

One of my last thoughts was of the captain, who had so often strode along the beach with his cocked hat, his sabre-cut cheek, and his old brass telescope. Next moment we had turned the corner, and my home was out of sight.

The mail picked us up about dusk at the Royal George on the heath. I was wedged in between Redruth and a stout old gentleman, and in spite of the swift motion and the cold night air, I must have dozed a great deal from the very first, and then slept like a log up hill and down dale through stage after stage; for when I was awakened at last, it was by a punch in the ribs, and I opened my eyes to find that we were standing still before a large building in a city street, and that the day had already broken a long time.

Practice activities

1. In the context of this extract, what does the word "mail" mean? Circle **one** answer.

      letters   **post**   **coach**   **armour**

2. Explain the meaning of the word "broken" in the words "the day had already broken a long time".

_____

_____

Test-style questions

1. Who had a cocked hat? Circle **one** answer.

      Jim   **the captain**   **Redruth**   **George**   *1 mark*

2. Where is the Royal George? Circle **one** answer.

      on the heath   **by a large building**   **near his home**   *1 mark*

3. What time of day were they travelling and how do you know?

_____

_____

2 marks

4. The word "stage" is used in the phrase "stage after stage". Write the meaning of the word "stage" as used in the extract, as well as another meaning of the word.

Meaning 1: _____

Meaning 2: _____

2 marks

Asking questions

Key to comprehension

When you are reading a text, it is vital that you ask yourself **questions** in order to understand it in more depth. Questions should focus on what the author is trying to achieve and the effect that the text has on you, the reader.

For example:
- How do I feel about the characters?
- What does the author want me to think about the characters?
- Do the author and the narrator (the character telling the story) feel the same way?
- Why is the author telling me this now?

Comprehension material

That House

Everyone seemed to avoid going anywhere near the huge old mansion at the top of the hill. In its former days it had been the thriving house of a rich family with a full set of servants; but tragedy had hit the family and they had moved away, leaving the mansion deserted, rundown, a shell of its former self.

Nobody really knew the details of the tragedy, except that it involved a dark, stormy night and the death of the master of the house from a "fall" from the rooftop. It was probably because of these events that people believed the house to be haunted. It was said that the ghost of the master roamed the corridors and made howling noises in the middle of the night.

I had heard these rumours from as young as I can remember. As a young girl I liked to believe them and scared myself at night with the thought that I could hear the howl of the man coming from the house. My friends believed it too, and I guess it was them that led me to be standing at the front door that day, on the fortieth anniversary of the tragedy.

I no longer believed the rumours and was going to prove that the house was nothing more than that, a house. I was going to stay the night – alone. I had my camera and my night things, and I was going to prove what really happened that fateful night and dispel the myth about ghosts.

Practice activities

1. In which paragraph does the narrator tell you why she was at the house?

   first   **second**   **third**   **fourth**

2. Why do you think this information is given after you have learnt about the history of the house and what her friends think about it?

   Tick **two**

   It makes you realise how brave she is.

   It means you cannot predict what will happen.

   The author had to do it that way.

   It sets the scene before she arrives.

Test-style questions

1. When the narrator is at the door, how many years is it since the tragedy? Circle **one** answer.

   4   **14**   **40**   **44**   *1 mark*

2. How do you feel about the narrator's friends? Use evidence from the text.

   _____

   _____

   _____
                                                       2 marks

3. Write a question that you could ask the narrator about herself.

   _____

   _____
                                                       1 mark

Drawing inferences

Key to comprehension

An **inference** is a conclusion based on evidence
and reasoning.

- For instance, if you are told, "The boy looked at his watch and then ran to the bus stop", you can infer that he is running because **he is late** even though you have not been told this.
- On the other hand, if you are told, "The boy looked over his shoulder back down the alley and then ran to the bus stop", you can infer he is **running away** from someone or something.

In both cases you have used the **evidence** available and **reasoning** (based on your knowledge of a range of different situations) to draw your own conclusion.

Comprehension material

Extract from *Grandpa Chatterji* by Jamilla Gavin

One day, Mum said excitedly, "Children! Your grandpa is coming to stay! Isn't that wonderful!" But they didn't think it was wonderful at all. Neetu groaned and said, "Oh no! I'll have to wear nothing but dresses," and Sanjay moaned, "Oh no! We'll have to eat curried eggs."

It was Dad who beamed at them and said, "It's not my dad from Leicester who's coming to visit us, it's your Mum's dad from Calcutta. You've never met him! You can call him 'Grandpa Chatterji'."

Neetu and Sanjay looked at each other doubtfully. How could they know whether a granddad from Calcutta was any different from a granddad from Leicester, even if he was called Grandpa Chatterji? They would just have to wait and see.

All that week Mum went round with a smile on her face, and even Dad seemed quite relaxed. Mum got the spare room ready, just as she always did for Dad's dad. But instead of worriedly scrubbing and cleaning and polishing and checking that there was not one speck of dust to be seen anywhere in the house, she actually hummed and sang and seemed to enjoy making everything look nice.

On the day of his arrival, Mum and Dad got up very early and drove off to the airport to meet Grandpa Chatterji. Neetu and Sanjay didn't go because there wouldn't be room in the car on the way back.

Practice activities

1. What can you infer from this extract about the granddad who lives in Leicester?

    _____

    _____

    _____

2. Which two countries do the children's grandfathers live in?

    _____ and _____

Test-style questions

1. What does Neetu say she will have to wear whilst her granddad is staying?
    Circle **one** answer.

    saris   **trousers**   **dresses**   **fancy dress**   *1 mark*

2. Who does not like eating curried eggs? Circle **one** answer.

    Mum   **Sanjay**   **Dad**   **Neetu**   *1 mark*

3. How do you think Mum felt about her dad coming to stay? How do you know?

    _____

    _____

    2 marks

4. How do you think the children might feel when they meet their granddad for
    the first time? Give reasons for your answer.

    _____

    _____

    2 marks

Justifying inferences

When you have used the evidence available to make an inference about something in the text, you then need to **justify** your reasoning. That is to say, you need to explain why you have come to that conclusion. This is a key skill to develop and one that is not difficult. It simply relies on identifying the evidence that you used to make your inference. Quoting the specific evidence from the text can be the best way of doing this.

Comprehension material

Extract from *The Balaclava Boy* by Richard Parkyn

The tyre blew instantly, the bus lurched violently. Mr Squires did the best he could, it was the best anyone could have done in the circumstances, but for a split second, he lost control. It hit the curb with the exact amount of force required to topple it over onto its side.

Children were thrown everywhere, the Shillabers included. Screams pierced the air. The bus scraped along the road with a horrific din of metal and glass on tarmac. Inside, the air was filled with sparks, smoke and the smell of burning rubber. Shards of glass pinged in all directions. An almighty crash added to the cacophony as the bus ploughed through the flyover railings and skidded for what seemed like an eternity before finally grinding to a halt.

A split second of icy stillness ended as the tumult resumed with greater panic. The bus was balanced precariously on the edge of the flyover and rocked eerily like a giant red seesaw. Black smoke bellowed from the back end.

Below on the A30, cars and trucks skidded to a halt in front of the fallen debris. The cars near the front reversed to a safe distance as a dozen mobile phones began ringing the emergency services. At this point there had been no serious injuries, but if the bus fell, that would certainly change.

Jack, Nigel and Sarah scrambled to check on each other first. They were all OK except for a few cuts and bruises on Nigel and Sarah.

Practice activities

1. What surname do Jack, Nigel and Sarah have?

_____

2. Where do you think the shards of glass that "pinged in all directions" came from? Give reasons for your inference.

_____

_____

_____

Test-style questions

1. Which road was the bus hanging over? Circle **one** answer.

A303   **A30**   **M5**   **A3**   _1 mark_

2. Two similes are used in this extract. Quote **one** of them below.

_____

1 mark

3. Describe the contrast between paragraphs 2 and 3. Give examples of how the author creates this contrast.

_____

_____

_____

_____

_____

3 marks

Using evidence from the text

Key to comprehension

When answering questions, it is important that you back up your answers with **evidence from the text**. This can be done in different ways, for example:
- The text says the girl pulled a face behind her friend's back, so she is not nice.
- The text says, "Lottie pulled a nasty face behind her friend's back", so we know that she is not being kind to her friend.

Comprehension material

Extract from *The Case of the Missing Stamp* by Dina Anastasio

"Pleasant afternoon," Fred said, leaning against Sam's old apple tree.

"Sure is," Sam said, as he placed a flower bulb gently into the soft earth. "Spring is in the air, all right."

Fred glanced about him.

"Look at that," he said. "What's up there? Looks like a bird is building a nest on your chimney."

Sam pulled himself to his feet and studied the top of his house. As he watched, a mother bird carried a small piece of straw over to the chimney and wrapped it into her nest.

"Ah yes," Fred went on. "Spring is certainly here."

Sam knelt down and dug into the earth – hard. He wished that Fred would go away and leave him alone. Fred would go on and on about spring and birds and nests and then, just like he always did, he'd start talking about stamps, stamps, stamps. Fred's favourite subject was stamps.

Fred took another deep breath, and walked over to Sam.

"Listen," Fred said, stepping on Sam's newly planted bulb. "You didn't happen to see an envelope did you?"

"Not that I can remember. What kind of envelope was it?"

"Just a plain white one. I left it here this morning when I stopped by for tea. My brother sent it to me. It had a rare Churchill stamp on it – cancelled last week."

"I don't pay much attention to stamps," Sam muttered.

"Hmmm, I know I had it when I stopped by. As a matter of fact, I'm pretty sure I left it on the kitchen table when we were having tea."

"Valuable stamp, was it?" Sam asked.

"Very valuable. It is very rare. There was a flaw in the hair. I really need it for my collection."

"It sounds interesting, but I'm afraid I haven't seen it."

Fred stepped backwards and turned towards the house, "You don't mind if I look on the table, do you?" he asked. "Just in case."

"Well," Sam said, "there's really no point, I did a bit of spring cleaning right after you left, and I'm afraid I threw everything into the fire. If your envelope was there, it's gone now."

Fred walked towards the door and opened it.

"I know you're lying," he said…

Using evidence from the text

Practice activities

1. When Fred is talking to Sam, what does he notice on the chimney?

   _____

2. What does Sam claim he did after Fred left earlier that morning? How does Fred know he must be lying?

   _____

   _____

   _____

Test-style questions

1. What does Fred say is "certainly here"? Circle **one** answer.

   birds   **spring**   **autumn**   **thieves**   *1 mark*

2. Where does Fred say he is "pretty sure" he left the envelope? Tick **one**.

   on the kitchen table ☐

   in the chimney ☐

   in the flowerbed ☐

   in the porch ☐   *1 mark*

3. Why do you think Sam wanted to keep the envelope? Explain your answer using evidence from the text.

   _____

   _____

   _____

   2 marks

Prediction

Key to comprehension

As you begin to read different books by different authors, you will find it easier to **predict** what might happen in a story. Authors give clues during the story, which means that you can make predictions, based on evidence from the story, and using knowledge of similar stories.

Some stories (like fables) are enjoyable because you often know what is going to happen. Other stories (like murder mysteries) are enjoyable because they surprise you.

Comprehension material

Extract from *The Monkey and the Bear*

A mighty bear was travelling through a great forest when he strayed off the path, convinced he could find a shorter way out of the trees. Time passed and, reluctant to admit his mistake the bear pressed on through the undergrowth, becoming more and more lost.

As he wandered about looking for a track to follow, he was eventually joined by a tiny monkey who swung through the branches above him, chattering away. Bear, absorbed in searching for a way out of the forest and dismissive of such a tiny creature, ignored his companion.

"I think you need my help," said Monkey, finally.

"Don't be ridiculous!" stormed Bear. "How could a tiny thing like you help a powerful bear like me? Why, you're so small you would fit in one of my paws!" Bear raised a huge paw and flashed its sharp claws at the monkey, who darted into the trees and disappeared. Bear chuckled and continued on his way, confident that he would shortly find a track that would lead him directly out of the forest.

Darkness fell and still Bear wandered in circles through the forest, with no idea where he was or what direction he was walking in. Although he trampled many miles that night, sunrise saw him back where he had started, tired, hungry and even grumpier than usual. He sat on a fallen tree and fumed, wondering how a mere forest could outsmart a mighty creature like him.

"I think you need my help," piped a little voice in the branches above.

Practice activities

1. Which other animal fable (with a moral) does this remind you of, and why?

   _____

   _____

2. What do you think will happen in the end?

   _____

   _____

Test-style questions

1. What **adjective** does the bear use to describe himself when talking to the monkey? Circle **one** answer.

   tiny   **powerful**   **mighty**   **huge**   *1 mark*

2. Which words are used instead of 'said'? Circle **two** answers.

   shouted   **stormed**   **piped**   **cried**   *2 marks*

3. What can a monkey do, that a bear cannot, that would help it find a way out of the forest? Explain your answer using evidence from the text.

   _____

   _____

   2 marks

4. What important lesson do you think the bear might learn by the end of the story?

   _____

   _____

   2 marks

Characters

Key to comprehension

Characters play a vital role in any fiction text, and **characterisation** can be quite subtle. For instance, good authors will not simply say that a character is "brave" or "greedy"; instead, they will show the character behaving in ways that make you realise this for yourself.

Comprehension material

Extract from *Yacht Rescue*

Lucy banged her bedroom door shut, a little harder than was strictly necessary, and flopped down on her bed. It wasn't fair! They just didn't understand her. Making sure they could hear her anger from downstairs, she kicked the headboard of her bed then sat up, sulkily.

It had been raining for weeks and this was the first really warm, dry evening of spring. Everyone had planned to meet in the park this evening. Most of them would be there already but where was she? Stuck at home, that's where. The worst of it was that Lucy knew she really only had herself to blame. Mum had said she could go, but that she had to be back by seven o'clock. Lucy had complained loudly that was too early, and before she knew what had happened, she had been sent to her room. Once again, her temper had let her down.

Lucy knew her parents would leave her to calm down and she probably wouldn't see them for the rest of the evening. Why keep her here if they weren't even going to spend time with her? She might as well not be here at all!

A thought began to form in Lucy's mind. Her bedroom window looked out onto the flat roof of the kitchen extension below. From there, she knew she could climb down onto the water butt, and down onto the patio. They would never know she had gone!

Wasting no more time, Lucy grabbed a jacket. She was safely on the patio and on her way to the park in a matter of moments.

The route to the park took Lucy along the seafront for a while and she slowed down to take in the view of the sea glistening in the late evening sunshine. Something on the horizon caught her eye. A small yacht bobbed on the sea in the distance. Lucy was no sailor but something about the vessel just didn't look right, even from this distance. Lucy wondered what to do. She had left her mobile phone charging at home, but even if she had it with her, did she really want to alert the coastguard when she wasn't really sure that anything was wrong?

Practice activities

1. What do you learn about Lucy's personality from this extract?

_____

_____

2. Based on what you know about Lucy, what do you think she might do? Explain your answer fully.

_____

_____

_____

Test-style questions

1. What time did Lucy's mum say she had to be back? Circle **one** answer.

   5.30pm   **8pm**   **7pm**   **6.30pm**   *1 mark*

2. In what order does she climb on these things? Start with **1** and label them in order.

   bedroom window ☐

   water butt ☐

   patio ☐

   kitchen extension ☐   *1 mark*

3. As well as not wanting to trouble the coastguard if nothing was wrong, why else might Lucy be reluctant to alert anyone?

   _____

   _____

   2 marks

Modern twists

Key to comprehension

Authors sometimes use a well-known traditional story to create their own modern, humorous version. This can be done in many ways. For example:

- by setting the story in a different time or culture
- by telling the story from a different character's viewpoint.

To fully understand these versions, it is important to know the traditional tales well.

Comprehension material

A Twist on "The Gingerbread Man"

Once upon a time an old woman ran a bakery. One evening, she decided to make a batch of gingerbread men, and when she was putting the finishing touches to the final one, he leapt up! She reached for him, but he was off, shouting, "Run! Run! As fast as you can! You can't catch me; I'm the Gingerbread Man!"

He jumped off the work surface and ran out of the bakery into the street, where he bumped into a little boy. "You look like a tasty snack," said the boy.

"Run! Run! As fast as you can! You can't catch me; I'm the Gingerbread Man!" he said, as he jumped onto a passing bus.

A little girl was playing on her iPhone on the bus. She looked up at the Gingerbread Man, rubbed her eyes to check that she was not imagining things and said, "You look very yummy!"

But the Gingerbread Man jumped off the bus shouting, "Run! Run! As fast as you can! You can't catch me; I'm the Gingerbread Man!"

Soon he came to a bridge over a wide river. A man was sitting on a scooter. He looked at the Gingerbread Man and said, "You look tired. Can I give you a lift across the river on my scooter?"

The Gingerbread Man asked, "Don't you want to eat me?"

"I can't, as I have an allergy to biscuits," the man replied. The Gingerbread Man was relieved and climbed up behind the man on the scooter.

Half way across the bridge, the man said to the Gingerbread Man, "There's not much room back there. Climb up onto my back." The Gingerbread Man clambered onto the man's back.

A little while later, the man said, "You're slipping down. Climb up onto my crash helmet." The Gingerbread Man clambered up onto the man's helmet.

Nearly at the end of the bridge, the man said, "You're slipping there too. Climb onto my nose." The Gingerbread Man clambered up onto the man's nose.

As the scooter got to the end of the bridge, the man flipped his head up. The Gingerbread Man sailed into the air, before plummeting down into the man's open mouth. CRUNCH! The man ate the Gingerbread Man in one bite.

Practice activities

1. What is the author relying on the reader already knowing to enjoy this?

   _____

2. Write down three modern items used in this story, that are not included in the traditional tale.

   a) _____

   b) _____

   c) _____

Test-style questions

1. Write down one example of a phrase used in this story that is often used in traditional stories.

   _____

   _____

   1 mark

2. What were they crossing on the scooter? Circle **one** answer.

   a market   **a street**   **a square**   **a bridge**   *1 mark*

3. Why did the Gingerbread Man trust the man not to eat him?

   _____

   1 mark

4. What did the man on the scooter lie about to the Gingerbread Man? Why did he lie?

   _____

   _____

   _____

   3 marks

Language and meaning

Key to comprehension

When a book is written about life in another culture, the **language** contributes strongly to setting the scene and can help readers learn about that culture. It may be that there are different words used for everyday objects, or that the language spoken by the characters contains some of the authentic language of the culture. For example:

- A novel set in the USA might talk about dimes (small coins), sidewalks (pavements) and bellhops (hotel porters).
- A novel set in India might talk about rupees (coins), ashrams (spiritual retreats) or chai wallahs (sellers of tea).

Comprehension material

Extract from *Journey to Jo'burg* by Beverley Naidoo

"Dineo is very ill, Mma," Naledi spoke between sobs. "Her fever won't go away. Non and Mmangwane don't want to trouble you, but I told Tiro we must come and bring you home."

Mma gasped again and held her children more tightly.

"Madam, my little girl is very sick. Can I go home to see her?"

The Madam raised her eyebrows.

"Well Joyce, I can't possibly let you go today. I need you tonight to stay in with Belinda. The Master and I are going to a very important dinner party…"

She paused.

"But I suppose you can go tomorrow."

"Thank you, Madam."

"I hope you realize how inconvenient this will be for me. If you are not back in a week, I shall just have to look for another maid, you understand?"

"Yes, Madam."

The children couldn't follow everything the Madam was saying in English, but her voice sounded annoyed, while Mma spoke so softly. Why does the white lady seem cross with Mma? It's not Mma's fault that Dineo is sick, Naledi thought.

ABOUT THE AUTHOR

Beverley Naidoo was born and grew up in South Africa, but now lives in England. She goes back to South Africa to stay in touch, especially with young people. A teacher for many years, she has a doctorate in education and a number of honorary degrees.

Journey to Jo'burg was her first children's book. It was an eye-opener for readers worldwide, winning awards, but it was banned in South Africa until 1991.

Practice activities

1. What do you think "Mma" means? How do you know this?

   _____

   _____

2. Why couldn't the children "follow everything the Madam was saying"?

   _____

   _____

Test-style questions

1. Where do you think this story is set? Circle **one** answer.

   South Africa   **India**   **England**   **USA**   *1 mark*

2. Give a reason for your answer to question 1, based on the information given.

   _____

   1 mark

3. What are the names of the mother's three children?

   _____   _____   _____   *3 marks*

4. Do you think the author wants us to like "Madam"?

   YES   **NO**   (circle **one**)

   Explain your answer fully using evidence from the text.

   _____

   _____

   _____

   3 marks

An author's use of structure

Key to comprehension

The **structure** of a text is carefully planned by the author. Fiction texts do not usually have obvious prompts (like sub-headings), however, the author has complete control of the order in which a reader finds out information. For instance, if they want to add a twist or surprise, they hold back information until their chosen moment. This can add to the suspense, interest and understanding of a text for the reader.

Comprehension material

Extract from *Jack and the Beanstalk*

Jack was a lazy boy who lived with his mother in the countryside. They did not have much money and what they did have only covered essentials. Jack was too lazy to help his mother or try to earn more money, even though he wanted the latest technology, clothes and music (which they could not afford).

One day Jack's mother decided that their funds were so low they would have to sell their only prize possession: Daisy the cow. She asked Jack to take the cow to market and get the best price he could for her. He refused. She then *told* him to take the cow to market and get the best price for her. He reluctantly got off the sofa, fetched the cow, and set off for market. However, he had not gone far when a small man appeared at his side (he seemed to have come from nowhere). The man offered Jack a pouch of magic beans in exchange for the cow. Jack leapt at the chance as it meant he didn't have to walk all the way to market.

When Jack arrived home his mum was furious. She threw the beans at him (they missed and sailed out of the window). She then sent him to bed with no dinner; partly because she was angry, and partly because she had no food to give him.

The next morning, Jack woke up even later than normal. Normally the daylight eventually woke him up, but today no light at all was shining through the window into his room. Jack could not understand what was happening. He opened his curtains; still no light. He walked into the sitting room and no light was coming in there. He tried to open the front door; it wouldn't move – not even a little bit. Jack's first thought was that his mother was so angry with him that she had locked him in and left. He called her name. She came running into the room shouting about everywhere being dark. He tried the back door and, when it opened, he crept out into the garden holding a bat to defend himself against the aliens that he had assumed had landed on Earth!

He did not expect to see what he did. The biggest, most enormous beanstalk filled the garden, reaching up and through the clouds. Its branches were leaning against the doors and windows preventing them from opening…

An author's use of structure

Practice activities

1. What information does the author give you straight away about Jack?

   _____

   _____

2. How does the author build suspense before Jack opens the back door?

   _____

   _____

   _____

Test-style questions

1. Which door could Jack not open? Circle **one** answer.

   trap door   **front door**   **cellar door**   **back door**   *1 mark*

2. In your own words, explain why Jack did not wake up at the usual time.

   _____

   _____

   2 marks

3. From the information in this extract, do you think that Jack should have swapped the beans for the cow?

   YES   NO   (circle **one**)

   Explain your answer using evidence from the text.

   _____

   _____

   _____

   2 marks

Presentation and meaning

Key to comprehension

It is important, even when you become a good reader, to still use pictures (where there are any) to help you infer and deduce what an author wants you to know. The text in comic strips, graphic novels and picture books will often not describe how things **look**. You therefore need to look carefully at the images, which can reveal a number of things. For example:

- Facial expressions and body language tell you how a character feels.
- General appearance and clothing can tell you something about a character and their role and position in life.
- Background detail tells you about the world in which the characters live.

Comprehension material

Extract from *Collins Big Cat – Tig in the Dumps* by Michaela Morgan

He didn't need anyone to remind him. How could he forget?

His mum had gone to lots of trouble to make his costume. She always tried her best at things. She'd made him a tiger costume. But she'd made one tiny mistake.

Can you spot it?

Presentation and meaning

Practice activities

1. What mistake does the picture show his mum has made with the costume?

   _____

2. How does the boy feel as he remembers wearing the costume? How do you know?

   _____

   _____

Test-style questions

1. In the picture that shows him wearing the costume, what does the boy's facial expression tell you he is feeling? Circle **one** answer.

   pride　　　**excitement**　　　**embarrassment**　　　**terror**　　　*1 mark*

2. Was the boy's mum trying to make him feel this way when she made the costume? How do you know?

   _____

   _____

   _____

   2 marks

3. The text says, "How could he forget?" What could he not forget and why did he not need reminding?

   _____

   _____

   _____

   2 marks

Setting the scene

Key to comprehension

The senses are very important when writing. Authors can use a lot of detail to paint an evocative picture in the heads of their readers. The following are often very important in setting the scene:

- shapes
- colours
- dimensions
- sounds
- smells
- textures.

Top tip

Use a dictionary to find out the meaning of unfamiliar words.

Comprehension material

Extract from *The Little Mermaid* by Hans Christian Andersen (translation by H.P. Paull)

Far out in the ocean, where the water is as blue as the prettiest cornflower, and as clear as crystal, it is very, very deep; so deep, indeed, that no cable could fathom it: many church steeples, piled one upon another, would not reach from the ground beneath to the surface of the water above. There dwell the Sea King and his subjects. We must not imagine that there is nothing at the bottom of the sea but bare yellow sand. No, indeed; the most singular flowers and plants grow there; the leaves and stems of which are so pliant, that the slightest agitation of the water causes them to stir as if they had life. Fishes, both large and small, glide between the branches, as birds fly among the trees here upon land. In the deepest spot of all, stands the castle of the Sea King. Its walls are built of coral, and the long, gothic windows are of the clearest amber. The roof is formed of shells, that open and close as the water flows over them. Their appearance is very beautiful, for in each lies a glittering pearl, which would be fit for the diadem of a queen.

Practice activities

1. What are of "clearest amber" and what colour is amber? Use a dictionary if needed.

    _____

2. Identify two adjectives that are used in the description of the castle. Describe their effect on the picture that is created for the reader.

    _____

    _____

    _____

    _____

Test-style questions

1. What is in the deepest part of the ocean? Circle **one** answer.

    a castle   **a church**   **a shipwreck**   **cables**   *1 mark*

2. What is "clear as crystal" an example of?

    Tick **two**

    a simile   ☐

    a metaphor   ☐

    rhyme   ☐

    alliteration ☐   *2 marks*

3. What do you think a "diadem" might be?

    _____

    _____

    2 marks

Myths

Key to comprehension

Myths are ancient stories that often include gods and goddesses, talking animals and other supernatural characters. Myths can serve many purposes, for example:

- they can try to explain how the world was created
- they can try to explain spiritual truths
- they can try to explain the natural world.

Sometimes the word **myth** is used to mean something that is not true. However, many people believe that myths carry a lot of truth. Myths often use **symbols**. For example, a dove can symbolise hope, or a snake can symbolise evil.

Comprehension material

"Remembering Fire" from the Alabama Tribe

Bear owned Fire in the beginning. He and his people carried it with them whenever they went hunting or fishing or searching for honey.

One day, Bear and his people came to a forest, where thousands of acorns had fallen from the oak trees. Bear put Fire down and they started eating these amazingly tasty treats. They could not get enough and wandered deeper into the forest for more, forgetting all about Fire.

For a while Fire burnt happily, but eventually it had nearly run out of food. It died down more and more, until finally it was nearly out. "Feed me!" Fire shouted to Bear. However, Bear and his people were somewhere deep inside the forest and could not hear Fire.

Just then, Man was walking by. "Feed me!" Fire cried out desperately.

"Who are you?" asked Man.

"I am Fire. I give light and heat."

"What do you eat?" Man asked.

"Wood!" Fire shouted.

Man found some sticks and laid them on Fire so they pointed in the four directions – to the North, the West, the South and the East. Fire was delighted and began eating.

Man watched Fire and was pleased by the warmth it gave out and the dancing flames. He pushed the sticks into the centre of Fire as they burnt down, so Fire could keep eating.

After some time, Bear and his people came back to get Fire. Fire was furious and roared with such white heat that Bear and his people were terrified. "I don't know you!" Fire yelled at Bear. Bear and his people backed away. They never carried Fire again. Man does.

Practice activities

1. Which of the characters could be described as "supernatural" and why?

_____

_____

2. What do you think the message of this myth is?

_____

_____

Test-style questions

1. Who owned Fire at the beginning of the story? Circle **one** answer.

   Man   **Bear**   **Fire**   **the People**   *1 mark*

2. Why did Fire cry "desperately" at Man? How did it get in the situation it was in?

   _____

   _____

   _____

   2 marks

3. In how many directions did Man lay sticks on Fire? Circle **one** answer.

   1   **2**   **3**   **4**   *1 mark*

4. Was Fire right to leave Bear for Man? Explain your answer.

   _____

   _____

   _____

   2 marks

Legends

Like myths, **legends** are a very old form of literature. Whereas myths tend to describe timeless events before the world as we know it began, legends are set in the world of time we know.

Legends generally involve heroes who are human, though they may have superhuman powers and do battle with magical creatures. Sometimes legends might mix **literal** truth with **symbolic** truth. They can be interpreted in many different ways.

Comprehension material

Saint George and the Dragon

One day a dragon flew into the city of Silene and found the perfect place to make its nest. Unfortunately, for the people of the city, this was right next to the spring where they got their water. Their simple life was now shattered. Many of the men of the city died fighting the dragon, but all to no avail.

The people of Silene decided that a different approach was necessary. They began to distract the dragon by giving him sheep to eat. Whilst he was eating, they were able to get the water they needed. But only for a short time, because they ran out of sheep to give to him!

The people could not survive without water and realised that they needed another plan. One of the city elders suggested the dragon could be fed young women instead of sheep! With no other plan, and now in desperate need, the people of Silene agreed. Their plan worked and the people drew lots each day to decide which girl would be sent next to the dragon.

One day, because the girls were picked at random, the princess of Silene was chosen to feed to the dragon! The king was distraught, but the princess wanted to be treated the same as the other girls in the kingdom. She walked, as bravely as she could, to meet the dragon.

As she stood in front of the terrible creature, Saint George rode by on his horse. He saw the pretty princess and realised immediately the danger she was in. He charged at the dragon and fought bravely and gallantly until the dragon lay dead. The Princess was saved! The people of Silene were in awe of Saint George's bravery and they converted to Christianity to be like him.

Practice activities

1. Who is the hero of the legend?

_____

2. What type of character is Saint George? Can you identify a character from another story who saves a girl / lady?

_____

_____

Test-style questions

1. What did the dragon make its nest next to? Circle **one** answer.

a spring   **a cave**   **a forest**   **a mountain**   *1 mark*

2. Why did the Silene people take sheep to be eaten by the dragon?

_____

_____

1 mark

3. What two adverbs are used to describe how Saint George fought?

_____   _____   *2 marks*

4. Who do you think was more brave – Saint George or the princess? Explain your answer.

_____

_____

_____

1 mark

Structure of play scripts

Key to comprehension

A **play script** is a piece of writing that is intended to be performed. In the same way that a novel is often divided into chapters, a play is often divided into **scenes**. Often there will be a list of characters at the start of the play script, and each scene that follows will usually consist of the following:

- **Dialogue** – What each character says placed to the right of their name. A new line begins when a new character speaks.
- **Stage directions** – Instructions, usually in italics, about how characters should speak and move and how props and scenery should be used. Stage directions are often put in brackets when inserted into the middle of dialogue.

Top tip

Learn the key features of play scripts so that you can write your own.

Comprehension material

Extract from *Little Red Riding Hood*

Characters
Little Red Riding Hood (LRRH)   Mother   Wolf   Granny   Huntsman

Scene 1
*The scene is the interior of a cottage with a forest that can be seen through the window. **LRRH** and **Mother** are already on stage. **Mother** is holding a basket. **LRRH** is sitting at the table finishing her breakfast.*

LRRH   It is such a shame that Granny is poorly. She was going to take me to see the animals at the zoo. *(sighing and putting her head in her hands)*

Mother   I know dear, but you will be able to go another time *(patting **LRRH** on the head in sympathy)*. I always wonder why you are so fond of all those animals!

LRRH   *(animated and standing up from the table to show excitement)* They are fascinating, Mummy! Every time we go I learn new things about them, although I think that the wolves are the most interesting of all…

Mother   *(interrupting)* Wolves! They give me the shudders. I am sure there are some that live in the woods.

LRRH   Wow! Really? I would love to meet one.

Mother   No you wouldn't. Not in the wild! Anyway, I have a job for you to do today: I have made some lovely cakes for Granny to cheer her up *(folding back the tea towel on top of the basket to show **LRRH** the cakes)*. Please can you take them to her and make sure there is nothing else she needs?

LRRH   Yes, of course Mummy. It will be such fun to see her too.

Mother   Don't forget to wear your cloak to keep warm and remember do *not* talk to anyone you meet that you don't know…especially not any wolves! *(laughing)*

Practice activities

1. Why is the character list included at the beginning?

   _____

2. List three layout features from the play script and write how each of these helps the actors.

Layout feature	How it helps

Test-style questions

1. How does Mother show sympathy to Little Red Riding Hood?

   _____

   1 mark

2. What do the letters LRRH mean and why have they been used?

   _____

   _____

   2 marks

3. Why does mother say that Little Red Riding Hood would not want to meet a wolf "in the wild"?

   _____

   _____

   2 marks

Characterisation

Key to comprehension

Characterisation is the way that an actor plays a role, using his or her acting skills to bring a character to life. Actors can be very creative in the tone and emotion they bring to their lines.

Body language (the way they walk and move) is also very important, and actors need to think about how they react to events on stage even when they are not speaking themselves.

Comprehension material

Extract from *A Typical Morning*

Characters: Mum   Dad   Eliza   Freddie

Scene 1

*Disorganised living room in family home. **Eliza** wandering around as if searching for something, looking cross. Seated at a table: **Dad** (reading newspaper) and **Freddie** (eating cereal).*

Eliza	*(angrily with her hands on her hips)* It is *not* funny, Freddie! Give me my PE kit back.
Freddie	*(in a voice that is trying not to laugh)* I don't have your PE kit. What would I want with a frilly, girlie skirt?
Eliza	*(exasperated)* You know it is not a skirt. It is shorts and a t-shirt just like you wear. Now… give… it… back.
Dad	*(without looking up from his newspaper)* What are you two arguing about now?

*Freddie and **Eliza** both begin telling him their side of the story at the same time.*

Dad	*(laughing)* I can't possibly hear you if you both speak at once! Try again.

*Freddie and **Eliza** both begin telling him their side of the story at the same time.*

Mum	*(hurrying into room still putting jewellery on and in a loud voice)* STOP! I could hear you two squabbling from upstairs. Freddie give Eliza her PE bag back (**Freddie** *gets the bag from behind the sofa and gives it back to **Eliza***). Eliza come and sit at the table (**Eliza** *sits down*), and Dad, put the newspaper down so that we can have breakfast as a family… quietly (**Dad** *puts the paper on the floor*). Now, what are you all doing today?

*Freddie, **Eliza** and **Dad** all begin talking at once.*

Mum	*(with her fingers in her ears and shouting)* AAAAAGGGGGGGGGGHHHHH! *(laughing and speaking normally)* Please, just one at a time! Eliza, you go first.

Answers

Pages 4–5
Practice activities
1. Ruth is a servant as she comes when the bell rings and she calls Mother "Mam". It tells us that it is set in a time when people in large houses had servants and rang bells to call them.
2. Father must have been telling them about what he did or what it was like when he was a boy.

Test-style questions
1. Told a story about a Princess (*1 mark*)
2. "Her dear face was as white as her lace collar" or "Her mouth looked like just a line of pale red" (*1 mark* for quoting either simile). The author is showing the reader how pale Mother has gone to emphasise how bad the news is (*1 mark* for explaining why the author has used the simile).
3. She wants to stop her saying any more in front of the children about what the bad news could be. (*1 mark*)

Pages 6–7
Practice activities
1. coach
2. The word means that the day had already started, i.e. the sun had risen over the horizon.

Test-style questions
1. the captain (*1 mark*)
2. on the heath (*1 mark*)
3. They were travelling overnight, as they got on the coach at dusk (evening) and he was woken when it was morning. (*1 mark* for stating at night; *1 mark* for using evidence from the text)
4. **Meaning 1:** a point in a journey / process (*1 mark*)
   Meaning 2: a platform where actors perform (*1 mark*)

Pages 8–9
Practice activities
1. fourth

2. It makes you realise how brave she is. / It sets the scene before she arrives.

Test-style questions
1. 40 (*1 mark*)
2. *Any plausible answer based on the text. For example:* I think they are sensible because they think the house is haunted and it probably is. / I think they are silly because they believe in ghosts. (*1 mark for a plausible response to the friends; 1 mark for using evidence from the text.*)
3. *Any plausible question based on the text. For example:* Why are you so interested in the house? / How old are you now? (*1 mark*)

Pages 10–11
Practice activities
1. The children do not like him. He likes Neetu to wear dresses. He likes eating curried eggs. He stays in the spare room when he visits. He makes Mum feel worried.
2. India and England.

Test-style questions
1. dresses (*1 mark*)
2. Sanjay (*1 mark*)
3. Relaxed and happy as it says she "hummed and sang" as she got everything ready. (*1 mark for correctly identifying her mood; 1 mark for using evidence from the text*)
4. Nervous and shy, as it says they have "never met him" and they doubt he will be different from their granddad from Leicester. (*2 marks for a plausible answer that is backed up with evidence from the text; 1 mark only for a plausible answer without evidence.*)

Pages 12–13
Practice activities
1. Shillaber
2. They came from the windscreen and windows of the bus. It says that "The

Answers

bus scraped along the road" and that the sound of "glass on tarmac" was heard.

Test-style questions

1. A30 *(1 mark)*
2. "skidded for what seemed like an eternity" / "rocked eerily like a giant red seesaw" *(1 mark for either answer)*
3. Paragraph 2 describes, in depth, the sounds during the initial crash, e.g. "horrific din of metal" and "almighty crash". In paragraph 3 there is "A split second of icy stillness", giving a contrast between noise and silence. *(3 marks for an answer that identifies the contrast between noise and silence with evidence from the text; 2 marks for using evidence from the text that shows some contrast but not the specific contrast of noise / silence; 1 mark for an answer that describes a contrast but with no evidence from the text.)*

Pages 14–15
Practice activities

1. a bird's nest
2. He says he was spring cleaning and threw everything into the fire. He couldn't have done this as the bird had made a nest on top of the chimney.

Test-style questions

1. spring *(1 mark)*
2. on the kitchen table *(1 mark)*
3. During the conversation Fred tells him that it is a "rare" and "valuable" stamp. Sam wants to keep it and sell it to make money, as he is not interested in collecting stamps. *(2 marks for answering that he wants to sell it and for noting that the text tells us it is rare and valuable; 1 mark only for answering he wants to sell it but omitting evidence from the text.)*

Pages 16–17
Practice activities

1. "The Lion and the Mouse", because the lion does not think a little creature like a

mouse can help him, but he needs the mouse's help in the end.
2. The monkey will help the bear to find his way out of the forest.

Test-style questions

1. powerful *(1 mark)*
2. stormed *(1 mark)*; piped *(1 mark)*
3. He can swing through the trees, which means he can see the way out. *(2 marks for an answer that links the swinging through the trees with being able to see the way out; 1 mark for an answer stating that he can swing through the trees but without making the link.)*
4. Bear will learn that even small creatures can help him and that being powerful is not the most important thing. *(2 marks for an answer that states both parts of the above; 1 mark for stating one part of the above.)*

Pages 18–19
Practice activities

1. She gets angry quickly and knows it; she sulks; she disobeys her parents; she is observant (she spots the yacht); she likes her own way; she is reckless; and she is inconsiderate.
2. *Predictions should be based on the evidence from her behaviour so far and the means available to her. For example: Perhaps she will be too selfish to help and will not want her parents to find out she has left the house.*

Test-style questions

1. 7pm *(1 mark)*
2. 1) bedroom window 2) kitchen extension 3) water butt 4) patio *(1 mark for all four in the correct order)*
3. She should not have been out of the house, so she might not want her parents to find out that she has sneaked out. *(2 marks for an answer that links not being allowed out and her parents finding*

2

out; **1 mark** for simply stating that she should not have been out of the house.)

Pages 20–21
Practice activities
1. The traditional story of "The Gingerbread Man".
2. bus; scooter; crash helmet; iPhone.

Test-style questions
1. "Once upon a time" (**1 mark**)
2. a bridge (**1 mark**)
3. He told him that he had an allergy to biscuits. (**1 mark**)
4. He lied about having an allergy to biscuits (**1 mark**), because he wanted to eat the Gingerbread Man (**1 mark**) and did not want to have to chase him (**1 mark**).

Pages 22–23
Practice activities
1. Mum / mother. The text says that she gasped and "held her children more tightly".
2. She is speaking in English and they only know a little English.

Test-style questions
1. South Africa (**1 mark**)
2. The author grew up in South Africa, so is writing about the culture she knows about. (**1 mark**)
3. Dineo, Naledi and Tiro (**1 mark** for each)
4. *Example answer:* **No**, because "Madam" behaves selfishly. She wouldn't let her maid go straight away to see her sick child and she said it was inconvenient. (**1 mark** for answering **No**; **1 mark** for each piece of evidence that supports an answer, whether **Yes** or **No**, up to maximum of an extra **2 marks**.)

Pages 24–25
Practice activities
1. That he lives with his mother in the country, does not help her, is poor but too lazy to work and wants the latest things.
2. The author builds suspense by not saying

what it is that is blocking the light, so the reader is left in the dark like Jack.

Test-style questions
1. front door (**1 mark**)
2. Something was blocking the window so the light could not come in to wake him up as usual. (**2 marks** for an answer that links something blocking the window with not waking up at the usual time; **1 mark** for stating that there was no light but without further explanation.)
3. *Example answers:* **Yes** because the man said that the beans were magic so they could bring them good luck; **No** because they still have no money and now have a giant beanstalk wrapped round their house! (**2 marks** for answers using evidence from the text; **1 mark** for answers with plausible reasoning but which do not use evidence from the text.)

Pages 26–27
Practice activities
1. Tigers have stripes, not spots.
2. Unhappy, because his facial expression is sad as he remembers the time he wore it.

Test-style questions
1. embarrassment (**1 mark**)
2. **No**, because the text says she had gone to "lots of trouble" to make his costume and "tried her best at things", and the picture shows her holding her son in a loving way. (**2 marks** for an answer that states **No** and gives evidence from the text and the picture; **1 mark** for an answer with evidence from the text or picture only.)
3. He could not forget the costume (**1 mark**) because it embarrassed him so much (**1 mark**).

Pages 28–29
Practice activities
1. The castle windows are amber, which is an orange / yellow colour.
2. *Any two of the following adjectives:*

Answers

deepest / long / gothic / clearest / beautiful / glittering. The effect of these is to show that the castle is amazing and brightly coloured.

Test-style questions
1. a castle (**1 mark**)
2. a simile; alliteration (**1 mark** for each)
3. Something worn by a queen (actually a kind of crown) (**1 mark** for inferring it is something worn by a queen; **2 marks** for answering it is a kind of crown.)

Pages 30–31
Practice activities
1. Fire because he is able to talk, and Bear because he uses Fire.
2. *Many possible answers. For example:* Do not take things for granted (Bear took Fire for granted but Man did not).

Test-style questions
1. Bear (**1 mark**)
2. Fire cried out because it was dying and needed more wood (**1 mark**). Bear had forgotten about Fire. (**1 mark**)
3. 4
4. Yes (**1 mark**), because Bear had not looked after him properly and Man did. If Man had not come along, Fire would have died out. (**1 mark**)

Pages 32–33
Practice activities
1. Saint George
2. Knight / Hero. *Any example of a knight / hero who saves a girl / lady.*

Test-style questions
1. a spring (**1 mark**)
2. They wanted to distract him so that they could get water. (**1 mark**)
3. bravely / gallantly (**1 mark** for each)
4. *Individual choices. For example:* The princess was more brave because she faced the dragon knowing she would probably die. (**1 mark** for an answer with a plausible reason.)

Pages 34–35
Practice activities
1. To show how many characters are in the play and to help assign parts at the beginning.
2. *Any three of the following:*

Layout feature	How it helps
List of characters	You can see straight away how many performers you need.
Scene descriptions	You know how to lay out the stage and where people should stand.
Names of characters in bold	It is clear who needs to say which of the lines.
Stage directions in italics / brackets	They are different from the words spoken, so you can identify them as stage directions quickly.

Test-style questions
1. She pats her on the head. (**1 mark**)
2. It means "Little Red Riding Hood" (**1 mark**) and it is shortened so that there is more space for the dialogue. (**1 mark**)
3. In the zoo, wolves are in cages (**1 mark**), but in the wild they are roaming free and might attack her (**1 mark**).

Pages 36–37
Practice activities
1. *Example answer:* The stage direction "angrily with her hands on her hips" lets the actor know how Eliza is feeling at that moment and her body language.
2. He is not really interested in what they are saying.

Test-style questions
1. irritated (**1 mark**)
2. *Many possible answers. For example:* A sheepish facial expression could show that he is sorry. (**1 mark**)
3. She can hear them arguing from upstairs (**1 mark**) and wants to sort the problem out and have a peaceful, family breakfast (**1 mark**).

Answers

Pages 38–39
Practice activities
1. Act 5 Scene 7
2. *Any of the following:* Where the action takes place (in a field). / What noises are heard from off-stage (alarums). / When the actors (Macbeth and Siward) enter. / What the actors do (they fight and Siward dies).

Test-style questions
1. a battle (*1 mark*)
2. That he is not afraid of any man born from a woman. (*1 mark*)
3. No (*1 mark*), he says, "The devil himself could not pronounce a title / More hateful to mine ear." (*1 mark*)

Pages 40–41
Practice activities
1. dance
2. crowd; host
3. his memory / the picture in his head

Test-style questions
1. stars (*1 mark*)
2. All the daffodils together by the lake. (*1 mark*)
3. *Example answers:* "I wandered lonely as a cloud" / "Continuous as the stars that shine" (*1 mark*)
4. **Yes** (*1 mark*), because he says that when he pictures them in his mind his "heart with pleasure fills". (*1 mark for using evidence from the text.*)

Pages 42–43
Practice activities
1. It emphasises the colour of the tiger and gives a sense of fire / danger.
2. The rhyming couplets help the poem sound good as each couplet creates a different rhyming sound. It adds to the powerful structure of the poem, which reflects how powerful the tiger is.

Test-style questions
1. questions (*1 mark*)
2. Who could have made you? (*1 mark*)

3. Was whoever made the tiger pleased with it (*1 mark*), and did they also make the lamb? (*1 mark*)
4. *Example answer:* The poet gives the impression that the tiger is strong and frightening by using words such as "fearful". He also wonders about the "distant deeps" in which the tiger was created, and so gives an impression of how mysterious it is. (*1 mark for stating the impression that the poet gives of the tiger and 1 mark for backing this up with how it is achieved.*)

Pages 44–45
Practice activities
1. "Painted stations whistle by."
2. The train is travelling so fast that they whizz by the poet's window. They are not really charging – the train is.

Test-style questions
1. a tramp (*1 mark*)
2. It means that from the window of the carriage you only see things very briefly as you are travelling so fast. (*2 marks for a correct explanation that links the train's speed with the view; 1 mark for a less developed explanation.*)
3. brambles (2) daisies (3) cart (4) (*2 marks for all three correct; 1 mark for two correct.*)
4. The rhythm of the poem is repetitive and makes the reader read the poem fast, like the sound of a fast train. The rhyming couplets add to the rhythm and sense of pace as the train speeds up. (*1 mark for a plausible answer.*)

Pages 46–47
Practice activities
1. France, because the French word for five is *cinq* and it has five lines.
2. "Beyond the dancing forests" is personification because dancing is a human activity.

5

Answers

Test-style questions

1. 6 *(1 mark)*
2. haiku *(1 mark)*
3. "like a minnow in a stream" *(1 mark)*
4. BEAU|TY   MOUN|TAINS   O|VER   BLA|ZING
   (*2 marks* for all correct; *1 mark* for two or three correct.)

Pages 48–49
Practice activities

1. The first four lines in each poem are written as rhyming couplets. The last line in each poem rhymes with the first and second lines.
2. 5
3. They make the reader laugh as they are humorous.

Test-style questions

1. knees; fleas *(1 mark for each correct word)*
2. *Example answer:* There once was a girl named Rose / With silky long hair on her toes (*1 mark* for a word written to rhyme with Rose that makes sense.)
3. *Individual choices, but a plausible reason should be given. For example:* **No**, because the rhythm and rhyme are too light and airy. *(1 mark)*

Pages 50–51
Practice activities

1. A recount text, as it would have an opening about where you went and then describe the events in chronological order.
2. A discussion text, as it would be giving arguments for and against in a balanced way.

Test-style questions

1. instruction *(1 mark)*
2. A diary would use informal language, contractions and possibly slang, whilst a write-up of an experiment would use more formal and technical language. (*2 marks* for an answer that explains the language of both types of text; *1 mark*

for an answer that explains one of the text types.)
3. the life cycle of a butterfly *(1 mark)*

Pages 52–53
Practice activities

1. A persuasive text, because it is an advert that is trying to persuade people.
2. Buy the new Robot X87-b

Test-style questions

1. chores *(1 mark)*
2. "Why do it yourself when the X87-b can do it for you?" *(1 mark)*
3. No *(1 mark)* because it says "the updated model" *(1 mark)*.
4. *Individual answers but children must use evidence from the text.* (*2 marks* for an opinion that is fully backed up with evidence from the text; *1 mark* for an opinion with little supporting evidence.)

Pages 54–55
Practice activities

1. The council is planning to build new houses; Farr's Field has been used for sledging in winter.
2. To point out that it is not flat and therefore cannot be used instead of Farr's Field for team games.

Test-style questions

1. Hilltop Crescent *(1 mark)*
2. 30 *(1 mark)*
3. *Any two of the following:* the roads will struggle to cope and would become dangerous; the school and the doctor's surgery are already too busy; residents of her street will lose their view; the villagers enjoy using the field for recreation. (*1 mark for each reason up to a maximum of 2 marks.)*
4. cricket and football *(1 mark)*

Pages 56–57
Practice activities

1. Mercury
2. Because "The chemicals in its atmosphere

cause much of the Sun's light to be reflected back into space".

Test-style questions
1. 109 (*1 mark*)
2. 4 (*1 mark*)
3. It is the closest and easiest planet to get to (*1 mark*).
4. It provides all of the energy for life on Earth (*1 mark*), and without it "nothing would be able to survive" (*1 mark*).

Pages 58–59
Practice activities
1. *Any grammatically correct question that makes sense in the context of the text. It must be properly punctuated with a capital letter at the start and a question mark at the end.*
2. It gives extra information that is not vital to the text but is interesting.

Test-style questions
1. the consuls (*1 mark*)
2. "The Roman Republic was an extremely successful government." / The consuls were more "just" and more "careful and thoughtful" than the kings. (*1 mark for either answer.*)
3. *Many possible answers. For example:* The Roman Republic lasted for nearly 500 years. (*1 mark for a plausible fact.*)
4. They could help each other make good decisions. It did not allow one person to gain too much power. (*1 mark for each reason.*)

Pages 60–61
Practice activities
1. It is a recount text because it uses chronological order and has a brief introduction and conclusion.
2. It really needs a proper introduction at the beginning to let the reader know who went, when and why.

Test-style questions
1. Long Gallery (*1 mark*)
2. They were radio-controlled. (*1 mark*)
3. "Apparently" (*1 mark*)
4. It was successful from the student's point of view because he / she had fun playing and shopping. It was probably not so successful from the teacher's point of view because the student does not seem to have learnt very much or have been very interested in much of the house. (*1 mark for identifying the student had fun; 1 mark for suggesting the teacher may have had a different opinion; 1 mark for using evidence from the text.*)

Pages 62–63
Practice activities
1. A newspaper article or non-chronological report because it has columns, a headline, a first paragraph with key information and is non-chronological.
2. **Who is it about?** The Smiths and Tabs **What happened over a year ago?** Tabs went missing **When did something amazing happen?** Thursday morning

Test-style questions
1. Diane (*1 mark*)
2. "She is in great shape" (*1 mark*)
3. They want more pets to be microchipped. / It is a good business opportunity for them. (*1 mark for either answer.*)
4. An advert (*1 mark*), because they could advertise their services and their discount and get more customers. (*1 mark for explaining the possible benefits of an advert.*)

Pages 64–65
Practice activities
1. *Many possible answers. For example:* "How about washing up instead of using the dishwasher?" The effect is to make

Answers

the reader think about their own use of water.

2. "We should be ashamed of such waste, as water is a very precious commodity"

Test-style questions

1. 20 *(1 mark)*
2. Wash them in a bowl rather than under a running tap. *(1 mark)*
3. Turn the tap off when brushing. *(1 mark)*
4. *Example answers:* So that there is enough water to go around. / So that we can continue to live comfortably. *(1 mark for a plausible reason.)*

Pages 66–67
Practice activities

1. It says it is "the perfect day out for the whole family", but later it says, "Everyone aged 6+ can come", so if your family includes children under the age of 6, not all your family could take part.
2. online; over the phone

Test-style questions

1. *Example answers:* unique / exciting / fun-packed. It makes the reader think that the activities are exciting and encourages them to take part. *(1 mark for identifying a correct adjective; 1 mark for a suitable explanation of the effect that this has.)*
2. mid-air jumps; speedy zips *(1 mark for each)*
3. *Example answer:* A high-wire adventure in the trees. *(1 mark)*
4. *Individual answers but must be backed up with evidence from the text. (2 marks for a detailed answer using evidence from the text; 1 mark for an answer without using evidence from the text.)*

Pages 68–69
Practice activities

1. *Individual answers, but they should be backed up with information from the text as well as their own arguments if relevant.*

2. People have very different opinions on this matter, so the debate will not be concluded any time soon.

Test-style questions

1. Parents can contact their children; Children can communicate freely. *(1 mark for ticking both.)*
2. *Any plausible argument. For example:* Smartphones could be used to do research in class and to make notes. *(1 mark)*
3. The author implies that even if schools set rules, parents and children often break them. So even if the school says children are not allowed to bring their phones, the children may still bring them. *(2 marks for a correct explanation specific to the text; 1 mark for a correct explanation but not specific to the text.)*

Pages 70–71
Practice activities

1. The plans were sent to the wrong address, were handwritten (so difficult to read) and needed to be checked by the county architects.
2. The architect's plans need to be sent to the Planning Department, which needs to check them and issue a ticket of certification.

Test-style questions

1. Mr Grieves *(1 mark)*
2. continue *(1 mark)*
3. Not yet *(1 mark).* The Planning Department are essentially "in favour" but they need Mr Grieves to "clarify the drawings". *(1 mark for using the text to explain how they are essentially in favour.)*

Practice activities

1. How do the stage directions for Eliza help the actor to understand the character in more detail?

   _____

   _____

2. What does the stage direction "without looking up from his newspaper" tell us about Dad?

   _____

   _____

Test-style questions

1. What does "exasperated" mean? Circle **one** answer.

   irritated   **fearful**   **happy**   **sad**   *1 mark*

2. How could the actor playing Freddie show that he is sorry when he gives the bag back without saying the word "sorry"?

   _____

   _____

   1 mark

3. Why does Mum come downstairs before she has finished getting ready?

   _____

   _____

   _____

   _____

   2 marks

Shakespeare

Shakespeare wrote his plays about 400 years ago, but he is still considered by many to be the greatest **playwright** who ever lived.

In Shakespeare's plays, characters use old-fashioned language. However, you will often be able to guess what unfamiliar words mean from the rest of the script.

Shakespeare's characters sometimes speak in poetry, and you may begin to appreciate the rhythm and rhyme of the lines when you hear them read aloud.

Comprehension material

Extract from *Macbeth* by William Shakespeare

ACT V SCENE VII   *Another part of the field*

[Alarums. Enter MACBETH]

MACBETH   They have tied me to a stake; I cannot fly,
                     But, bear-like, I must fight the course. What's he
                     That was not born of woman? Such a one
                     Am I to fear, or none.

[Enter YOUNG SIWARD]

YOUNG SIWARD   What is thy name?
MACBETH   Thou'lt be afraid to hear it.
YOUNG SIWARD   No; though thou call'st thyself a hotter name
                     Than any is in hell.
MACBETH   My name's Macbeth.
YOUNG SIWARD   The devil himself could not pronounce a title
                     More hateful to mine ear.
MACBETH   No, nor more fearful.
YOUNG SIWARD   Thou liest, abhorred tyrant; with my sword
                     I'll prove the lie thou speak'st.

[They fight and YOUNG SIWARD is slain]

MACBETH   Thou wast born of woman
                     But swords I smile at, weapons laugh to scorn,
                     Brandish'd by man that's of a woman born.

Practice activities

1. What **act** and **scene** is this extract from? Use ordinary numbers rather than the Roman numerals in your answer.

   _____

2. In this extract, what kind of information do the stage directions give to the actors? Write down two different things.

   a) _____

   b) _____

Test-style questions

1. What is happening in this scene? Circle **one** answer.

   a battle   a feast   shopping   a game   *1 mark*

2. What does Macbeth claim?

   Tick **one**

   That he is the greatest king who ever lived. ☐

   That he is not afraid of any man born from a woman. ☐

   That Young Siward is a coward. ☐

   That he is not afraid of hell. ☐ *1 mark*

3. Does Young Siward enjoy hearing the name Macbeth? Explain your answer using a quotation from the text.

   _____

   _____

   _____

   2 marks

Figurative language

Key to comprehension

Figurative language is language that does not have a literal meaning.

For example, if you describe somebody as a star you do not mean they are literally a star, but that they are very special in some way. The word star is therefore being used figuratively or **metaphorically**.

Poets use a lot of figurative language, including:
- similes (e.g. she is like a star)
- metaphors (e.g. she is a star)
- hyperbole (e.g. I have a million things to do)
- personification (e.g. the sun is smiling).

Top tip

Learn each type of figurative language and the effect each one has on the reader.

Comprehension material

"I Wandered Lonely as a Cloud" by William Wordsworth

I wandered lonely as a cloud
That floats on high o'er vales and hills,
When all at once I saw a crowd,
A host, of golden daffodils;
Beside the lake, beneath the trees,
Fluttering and dancing in the breeze.

Continuous as the stars that shine
And twinkle on the milky way,
They stretched in never-ending line
Along the margin of a bay:
Ten thousand saw I at a glance,
Tossing their heads in sprightly dance.

The waves beside them danced; but they
Out-did the sparkling waves in glee:
A poet could not but be gay,
In such a jocund company:
I gazed—and gazed—but little thought
What wealth the show to me had brought:

For oft, when on my couch I lie
In vacant or in pensive mood,
They flash upon that inward eye
Which is the bliss of solitude;
And then my heart with pleasure fills,
And dances with the daffodils.

Practice activities

1. Which verb does Wordsworth use several times to personify the daffodils?

   _____

2. Which nouns in the first stanza make the daffodils seem like a group of people?

   _____

3. What does Wordsworth mean by his "inward eye"?

   _____

Test-style questions

1. What "twinkle on the milky way"? Circle **one** answer.

   daffodils   **trees**   **stars**   **waves**   *1 mark*

2. What was the "crowd" that Wordsworth writes about?

   _____

   1 mark

3. Quote a simile that is used in this poem.

   _____

   1 mark

4. Does Wordsworth like the daffodils?   **YES**   **NO**   (circle **one**)

   How do you know?

   _____

   _____

   _____

   2 marks

The sound of poetry

Key to comprehension

How a poem **sounds** is very important. Some poems are written to be read aloud, and even poems that are just written to be read make a sound in your mind as you read. Some of the most common techniques poets use to create sound effects in their writing are:

- rhyme (e.g. fat cat)
- rhythm (the beat you can hear in the words)
- repetition (repeating a word)
- alliteration (e.g. creeping cat, massive mountain).

Comprehension material

"The Tiger" by William Blake

Tiger! Tiger! burning bright
In the forests of the night,
What immortal hand or eye
Could frame thy fearful symmetry?

In what distant deeps or skies
Burnt the fire of thine eyes?
On what wings dare he aspire?
What the hand, dare seize the fire?

And what shoulder, and what art
Could twist the sinews of thy heart?
And when thy heart began to beat,
What dread hand? and what dread feet?

What the hammer? what the chain?
In what furnace was thy brain?
What the anvil? what dread grasp
Dare its deadly terrors clasp?

When the stars threw down their spears,
And water'd heaven with their tears,
Did he smile his work to see?
Did he who made the lamb make thee?

Tiger! Tiger! burning bright
In the forests of the night,
What immortal hand or eye
Dare frame thy fearful symmetry?

Practice activities

1. "Burning bright" is an example of alliteration. What effect does this create?

   _____

2. Rhyming couplets are used throughout this poem. What effect does this have on the poem's structure and message?

   _____

   _____

Test-style questions

1. What sentence type is repeated throughout the poem? Circle **one** answer.

   questions   **statements**   **exclamations**   **commands**   *1 mark*

2. In the first stanza, the speaker is asking who could "frame thy fearful symmetry?" What would be a simple way of asking this question?

   _____

   1 mark

3. Explain what the poet is saying in the last two lines of stanza 5.

   _____

   _____

   2 marks

4. What impression does the poet give of the tiger and which words / phrases create this effect?

   _____

   _____

   _____

   2 marks

Words in context

Key to comprehension

When reading poetry, you may sometimes encounter familiar words that are used in unfamiliar or surprising ways. It is important to look at the **context** in which the word appears when this happens, to understand its meaning. You can try the following:

• Look at the surrounding sentences.
• Think about the overall theme of the poem.
• Look at the poem's title – often the biggest clue is there.

Comprehension material

"From a Railway Carriage" by Robert Louis Stevenson

Faster than fairies, faster than witches,
Bridges and houses, hedges and ditches;
And charging along like troops in a battle
All through the meadows the horses and cattle:
All of the sights of the hill and the plain
Fly as thick as driving rain;
And ever again, in the wink of an eye,
Painted stations whistle by.
Here is a child who clambers and scrambles,
All by himself and gathering brambles;
Here is a tramp who stands and gazes;
And here is the green for stringing the daisies!
Here is a cart runaway in the road
Lumping along with man and load;
And here is a mill, and there is a river:
Each a glimpse and gone forever!

Practice activities

1. What happens in a "wink of an eye"?

_____

2. Why are the horses and cattle described as "charging along like troops in a battle"? Are they really charging?

_____

_____

Test-style questions

1. Who "stands and gazes"? Circle **one** answer.

   a farmer   **a tramp**   **a child**   **a witch**   *1 mark*

2. In your own words, explain what "each a glimpse and gone forever" means.

   _____

   _____

   2 marks

3. Sequence these things in the order in which they are mentioned in the poem. The first one has been done for you.

   brambles [ ]   daisies [ ]

   cart [ ]   child [1]   *2 marks*

4. How does the poet create a feeling of speed?

   _____

   _____

   _____

   1 mark

Types of poetry

Key to comprehension

There are many different forms of poetry, often reflecting different times and cultures. Many of them have particular structures that the poet is expected to follow. An English sonnet, for example, has the following key features:

- 14 lines
- 10 syllables to a line
- often about love
- often finish with an unexpected twist.

As you develop as a reader, it is important that you read a wide range of poetry, so that you can identify poetry in different forms.

Comprehension material

Haiku

Haikus originate in Japan. They have just three lines, are about nature and often contrast two things. Traditionally they have a syllable count of 5 / 7 / 5, but more recently they follow the idea that they are to be "expressed in one breath".

Fog in the air

lost

nature's beauty

Cinquain

Cinquains have five lines (*cinq* means "five" in French). The syllable pattern is 2 / 4 / 6 / 8 / 2.

Cool breeze,

Sparkling water,

Sun blazing on my back.

Golden sand between my warm toes…

the beach.

Tanka

Tankas are Japanese. They contain five lines with a syllable pattern of 5 / 7 / 5 / 7 / 7. They usually contain similes, metaphors or personification.

Over the mountains,

beyond the dancing forests.

The happy child swims,

in the sparkling cool water;

like a minnow in a stream.

Practice activities

1. Which country do you think the name **cinquain** came from? Explain why you think this.

_____

_____

2. Which line contains personification in the **tanka** poem? Why is it personification?

_____

_____

Test-style questions

1. How many syllables are there in the third line of a **cinquain**? Circle **one** answer.

     4   **2**   **6**   **8**   _1 mark_

2. Which type of poem often contrasts two ideas in nature? Circle **one** answer.

     tanka   **haiku**   **cinquain**   **sonnet**   _1 mark_

3. Quote the simile that has been used in the **tanka**.

_____

1 mark

4. Divide these words into their syllables using small vertical lines.

     B E A U T Y   M O U N T A I N S

     O V E R   B L A Z I N G

2 marks

Structure and meaning

Different types of poems, with their different **structures**, tend to suit different topics. For example:

- **Odes** and **sonnets** are suited to dealing seriously with topics such as love, death, truth, etc.
- **Haikus** and **cinquains** are very effective for making brief observations about nature.
- **Limericks** make effective use of rhythm and rhyme when a poet wants to make you laugh.

Comprehension material

Poem 1

There once was a sailor so hairy
That his beard and moustache were quite scary.
Strange mythical creatures
Roamed deep in his features,
Which made his poor barber quite wary!

Poem 2

There once was a girl named Louise
With silky long hair on her knees.
Her eccentric GP
Said that, "If you ask me,
You need to be treated for fleas!"

Practice activities

1. What do you notice about the rhyme patterns?

   _____

   _____

2. How many lines are there in each poem? _____

3. What is the effect of the last line in each poem?

   _____

   _____

Test-style questions

1. Which two words are used to rhyme with "Louise"?

   _____   _____

   2 marks

2. Write the first two lines of a poem, based on **poem 2**, where the girl is called **Rose** instead of Louise.

   _____

   _____

   1 mark

3. Do you think you could write something serious using the structure used in these poems?

        YES   **NO**   (circle **one**)

   Explain your answer.

   _____

   _____

   1 mark

Types of non-fiction

Key to comprehension

Non-fiction refers to a type of writing that is based on real-life events and facts, as opposed to fiction, which refers to events that are made up. In other words, non-fiction texts give the reader real-life information. They can be in many different forms and it is important to learn the main ones and their associated features.

Comprehension material

What type of text is it?

Recount Texts	Non-Chronological Reports
Purpose: To retell an event or series of events.	**Purpose:** To document information about a particular subject.
Features: Generally in chronological order; usually begin with an introduction and end with a conclusion.	**Features:** Often contain an opening statement, a conclusion, a series of facts using technical language, diagrams, photos and illustrations.
Examples: diary, journal, write-up of an experiment	**Examples:** encyclopaedias, topic-based books
Instruction Texts	**Discussion Texts**
Purpose: To tell someone how to make or do something.	**Purpose:** To discuss an issue or offer two or more points of view.
Features: Often contain headings, a list of materials and a step-by-step method using imperative verbs.	**Features:** Often contain arguments for and against, emotive language and a recommendation in the conclusion.
Example: instructions	**Examples:** newspaper articles, book reviews
Persuasive Texts	**Explanation Texts**
Purpose: To try to make readers agree with a point of view, to change their mind, or to encourage them to do something.	**Purpose:** To give an account of how or why something happens.
Features: Often contain strong opinions and adjectives, emotive language, emphasis through repetition, rhetorical questions and humour.	**Features:** Often contain technical language, diagrams and a question as a heading, and often describe processes and cause and effect relationships.
Examples: adverts, brochures	**Example:** explanation of the water cycle

Practice activities

1. If you were writing a text to tell people about a school visit you had been on, which type of text would you be writing? Explain your choice.

    _____

    _____

2. A text with the title "Should dogs be allowed in parks?" is which kind of text? Explain your answer.

    _____

    _____

Test-style questions

1. Which type of text is a recipe? Circle **one** answer.

    discussion   **argument**   **report**   **instruction**   *1 mark*

2. How would a **diary** (recount text) differ from a write-up of a **science experiment** (another recount text) in terms of the language used?

    _____

    _____

    2 marks

3. Which of the following would be classified as an **explanation** text?

    Tick **one**

    an advert for coffee   ☐

    installation instructions for a computer   ☐

    the life cycle of a butterfly   ☐   *1 mark*

Impact on the reader

Effective writing makes an **impact** on the reader. When you write a text you need to bear in mind who will be reading it and what its purpose is.

For instance, information texts should present the reader with details they want or need, making use of the facts and using images to help make things clear.

Adverts (a type of persuasive text) should make the reader want to buy the product or service by making it look attractive and by using emotive language.

Comprehension material

ROBOT X87-b

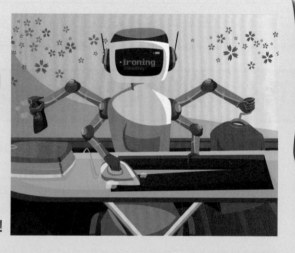

Do you need more help around the home?

Are you fed up of doing everything yourself?

Never fear! Robot X87-b has spun into the market and is now leading the way!

> *Why do it yourself when the X87-b can do it for you?*

He can be programmed to do household cleaning chores without the need for human intervention. This leaves time for you to have some YOU time.

Just click the programme you want him to perform, put your feet up and watch him work!

Improved technology
The updated model can perform 20 new chores!
Buy it now whilst stocks last.

Practice activities

1. What type of text is this? How do you know?

   _____

   _____

2. What does the text want you to do?

   _____

Test-style questions

1. What does the robot do that you might find boring? Circle **one** answer.

   homework   **eats**   **sleeps**   **chores**   *1 mark*

2. What slogan, in the form of a question, has been used?

   _____

   1 mark

3. Is this the first robot that this company has made? How do you know?

   _____

   _____

   2 marks

4. Does the text make you want to buy a Robot X87-b? Explain your answer clearly.

   _____

   _____

   _____

   _____

   2 marks

Facts and opinions

Key to comprehension

Facts are true pieces of information. For example, it is a fact that London is the capital of England.

Opinions are things which may not be true and are based on personal thoughts and feelings. For example, Isaac may think London is the best city in the world, whereas Uzma might think Edinburgh is.

Authors can often present their opinions as if they were facts. It is therefore important to be able to distinguish between facts and opinions.

Comprehension material

Head of Planning
Westport Town Council
Ring Road
Westport
Kent
WS19 5SL

11 Hilltop Crescent
Westport
Kent
WS13 4PN

20th December

Dear Sir,

I am writing to object very strongly to the plan to build houses on Farr's Field, Lower Buckham.

If 30 new houses are built on this land, the narrow local roads will struggle to cope with the extra traffic. Many of the lanes are not wide enough for two cars to pass each other and would be dangerous if they became any busier. Our school has no empty places and the doctor's surgery is always too busy already. Where will the people who buy these houses send their children to school, or see a doctor?

Houses like mine, which back on to Farr's Field, will lose their beautiful view and instead look out at row upon row of houses.

I know that there is a shortage of housing in the area, but Farr's Field has been used and enjoyed by the villagers for as long as any of us can remember. All year round it is used by ramblers and dog walkers and in the winter it provides some of the best sledging for miles around. The level area of the field is mown and used for football and cricket matches. The village park is lovely, but it slopes quite steeply in places, making it unsuitable for team games.

For these reasons, I am asking the council to turn down the application to build on this land.

Yours faithfully,

Ms Gowland

Practice activities

1. Which of these statements are likely to be **facts** rather than opinions?

Tick **two**

The council is planning to build new houses. ☐

The doctor's surgery is already too busy. ☐

The new houses will spoil the view. ☐

Farr's Field has been used for sledging in winter. ☐

2. What is the purpose of Ms Gowland mentioning the village park?

_____

_____

Test-style questions

1. Where does the author of the letter live? Circle **one** answer.

   Village Park   Farr's Field   Hilltop Crescent   Town Council   *1 mark*

2. How many new houses might be built on Farr's Field? Circle **one** answer.

   40   11   30   50   *1 mark*

3. Summarise two of the reasons that Ms Gowland gives for not wanting the houses built.

   a) _____

   b) _____

   2 marks

4. Which two sports are played on Farr's Field?

   _____ and _____   *1 mark*

Retrieving information

The purpose of non-fiction texts is to convey information to the reader, and often there is a lot of it. **Retrieving information** from texts is a bit like detective work; you will need good attention to detail as you look for the evidence you require.

Where a question carries more marks, you often need to quote evidence from the text in your answer. This may be needed to show how you have reached a conclusion about the text.

Top tip

Skim the text to look for key words that relate to the question.

Comprehension material

The Solar System

At the centre of our solar system is a star, the Sun. It is comprised of, amongst other things, hydrogen, helium, oxygen and carbon. It is approximately 109 times bigger than the Earth. The Sun is constantly undergoing a massive series of nuclear reactions, which give out an immense amount of heat and light.

The planet nearest the Sun is Mercury; so called because of its rapid orbit around the Sun (Mercury was the messenger of the Roman gods and very fast). Mercury has a surface which is similar in some respects to the surface of the Moon, in that it is cratered and inactive.

The second planet in the solar system is known as Venus (named after the Roman goddess of love). The chemicals in its atmosphere cause much of the Sun's light to be reflected back into space. This means that astronomers cannot see the actual surface of the planet. It also means that the planet appears to shine very brightly in the sky. For many centuries people believed that it was not a planet at all, but another star.

The third planet from the Sun is our own: Earth. As far as we know, it is the only planet in the galaxy to support life. Its distance from the Sun, coupled with its atmosphere and surface conditions, have meant that Earth is perfect for life to flourish. All energy used by life on Earth comes from the Sun at some point, and without the Sun nothing would be able to survive.

After Earth comes Mars (named after the Roman god of war). Mars is often nicknamed "the red planet" because it is covered with a layer of red rock and dust. Mars has received a great deal of interest from space agencies, owing to the fact that it is the nearest extraterrestrial destination – after the Moon – to which humans might travel. There have been several very successful probe landings on the surface of Mars, notably *Opportunity* and *Curiosity*.

Beyond Mars lies the rest of the solar system: another four planets, a dwarf planet, and all of their moons. The Sun's light eventually reaches them all, and then beyond them to the furthest reaches of space.

Practice activities

1. Who was the messenger of the Roman gods?

_____

2. Why does Venus appear to "shine very brightly in the sky"? Quote evidence from the text in your answer.

_____

_____

Test-style questions

1. Approximately how many times bigger is the Sun than Earth? Circle **one** answer.

    108   **100**   **109**   **101**   *1 mark*

2. How many planets are beyond Mars? Circle **one** answer.

    8   **5**   **4**   **2**   *1 mark*

3. Why are space agencies interested in Mars?

_____

_____

1 mark

4. Why is the Sun so important to life on Earth?

_____

_____

_____

2 marks

Asking questions

Key to comprehension

As you read, you should ask yourself **questions** about the text, its impact on you and the author's intentions. This helps you deepen your understanding and ensures that you do not always believe everything you read without question. Possible questions might be:

- Why has the author arranged the material in this way?
- What does this word mean?
- How do I feel about what the author is saying?
- Do I have a different opinion?

Top tip

Read around a subject to get more than one author's point of view.

Comprehension material

The Roman Republic

The Romans believed that their city was founded in the year 753 BC. However there is debate among modern historians who think that it is more likely to have been in 625 BC.

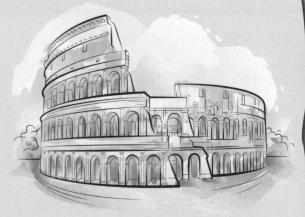

When Rome began it was governed by kings. However, after seven of these had ruled, the people decided that they did not want one person to have all the power. They also did not want their rulers to have power for too long. Therefore, in 509 BC Rome became a republic*. Each year, two consuls were elected. These men ruled for one year only, and could block each other's decisions if they thought they were wrong.

This meant that they were more just than the kings had been. They were also more careful and thoughtful rulers because they knew they could be punished by the new consuls who would take over after one year.

The consuls worked closely with a group of men in the senate. The senate had little power when the kings ruled, but they had much more influence over the consuls who often followed their directions.

The Roman Republic was an extremely successful government as it lasted for nearly 500 years!

* The word "republic" comes from the Latin words *res publica* which mean "public matters".

Asking questions

Practice activities

1. Write a question that you would like to ask the author (this could be about something else you would like to know about the Roman Republic, or something about the way the author has written the information).

_____

2. Why do you think the information in the footnote has not been placed in the main text?

_____

_____

Test-style questions

1. Who was elected each year? Circle **one** answer.

the king   **the senate**   **the republic**   **the consuls**   _1 mark_

2. Write down one example where the author has given an **opinion**.

_____

_____

1 mark

3. Write down one **fact** from the text.

_____

1 mark

4. What made it a good idea to have two consuls for one year?

_____

_____

2 marks

Structure and meaning

Key to comprehension

The way in which a non-fiction text is **structured** is determined by the type of text that it is. The main text types (see page 50) have features that help determine the structure. For example:

- **Recount texts** have an introduction followed by a description of events in a chronological order.
- **Report texts** have an introduction, key points and a conclusion, but do not have to be organised in chronological order.

Both of the above will normally use paragraphs to organise the information and make it easier to read.

Comprehension material

Our visit to Montacute House and Gardens

When we arrived, the coach had to drive along a very long driveway (just like it had been in Elizabethan times), so we got a really great view of the enormous house. The coach parked in front of the house and two guides met us. Their names were Martha and Robin. They took us into the house and through each of the rooms, starting on the ground floor. They told us that it would have had the Great Hall, kitchens and pantries on the ground floor and the retiring rooms on the upper floors. Martha and Robin talked a lot, but the Long Gallery at the top of the house was the best bit for me, as it was the biggest room I had ever seen. Apparently, the pictures were very old and famous, but the room was better!

After we had finished in the house, we had lunch. We all sat in the gardens at the back of the house as it was a sunny day. I was a bit fed up because my mum had accidentally put my sister's sandwiches in my lunchbag (tuna – yuck!), so I didn't eat them. We were then allowed to play for 15 minutes and had great fun as there was a huge tree swing that two of us could go on at once (Spencer was too scared to have a go though!).

When we had finished playing, we were taken on a tour of the gardens which were huge (I wish that my garden was that big!). There was so much grass that they had radio-controlled lawnmowers!

After the tour of the gardens, we went to the shop to spend our £5. I bought a really cool wooden ruler with all the kings and queens of England on it as well as a bag of sweets. Then, after everyone had been to the toilet, we got on the coach to go back to school.

I really enjoyed the visit, especially playing on the swing and spending my money in the shop. I hope we get to go on lots more school visits!

Structure and meaning

Practice activities

1. What type of text is this and how do you know?

    _____

    _____

2. What might be added to the beginning of the text to make it better?

    _____

    _____

Test-style questions

1. Which room has never been on the ground floor? Circle **one** answer.

    pantry   **Great Hall**   **Long Gallery**   **kitchen**   *1 mark*

2. What was unusual about the lawnmowers?

    _____

    1 mark

3. Which word shows that the author was not especially impressed that the pictures were old and famous?

    _____

    1 mark

4. Do you think the visit was successful from **both** the student's and the teacher's point of view? Use evidence from the text to back up your answer.

    _____

    _____

    _____

    _____

    3 marks

Presentation and meaning

Key to comprehension

How a non-fiction text is **presented** has a huge impact on the reader and their engagement with the text.

For instance, instructions will often have an equipment or ingredients list and then numbered, step-by-step instructions. This immediately lets readers know what type of text it is and highlights what they will need before they begin.

A newspaper article, on the other hand, is easily identified by often being written in columns, and by having a headline and a first paragraph that gives the reader key information.

Top tip

Look for key layout features to identify text types.

Comprehension material

Tabs comes home

DELIGHTED pet owners Martin and Diane Smith have been reunited with missing moggy Tabs, a whopping 17 months after she disappeared from their back garden.

Tabs reappeared in the Smiths' garden on Thursday morning to the amazement of the couple, who had given up any hope of seeing their pet again.

Diane Smith explains: "I was washing up, looked out of the window and there she was, just sitting in the garden. I couldn't believe it. We looked everywhere for her when she went missing. We put posters up, contacted the newspapers, even the local radio station. When we didn't find her, we assumed she must have been run over or locked accidentally in someone's shed."

Where Tabs has been for the past 17 months remains a mystery. "She is in great shape, so we think someone must

Tabs now back at home.

have been feeding and caring for her. We're just thrilled to have her back."

Now that she is safely back home, the Smiths are taking precautions to prevent Tabs from wandering off again. She stays in the house at night now, and has been microchipped. Mill House Veterinary Surgery, who take care of Tabs, are hoping that other pet owners will hear about Tabs and decide to have their pets microchipped too. They are offering the procedure at a reduced price next month.

Presentation and meaning

Practice activities

1. What type of text is this and how do you know?

    _____

    _____

2. Using the first and second paragraphs of the extract, answer these questions:

    Who is it about? _____

    What happened over a year ago? _____

    When did something amazing happen? _____

Test-style questions

1. What is Mrs Smith's first name? Circle **one** answer.

    Diana   **Dino**   **Diane**   **Tabs**   *1 mark*

2. Why do the Smiths think that Tabs has been looked after by someone?

    _____

    1 mark

3. Why do you think the vets are offering a reduced price for the microchipping?

    _____

    1 mark

4. What might Mill House Veterinary Surgery want to put on the same page as this article?

    Explain why they would do this.

    _____

    _____

    2 marks

Language and meaning

Key to comprehension

The type of **language** used in texts is often determined by the audience and purpose of the text. For instance, a description of a chemistry experiment will have scientific language, which will assume a knowledge of chemistry.

A persuasive text, on the other hand, may contain emotive language or rhetorical questions to make the reader come to the same conclusions as the author.

Top tip

Look out for emotive language that tries to create an emotional response in the reader.

Comprehension material

Saving water

Water is essential for life; to drink, to cook, to clean and so on. However, there is a limited supply of water on our planet. Each day, more people are being born and so the supply has to be shared among more people. We also expect a higher standard of living now, which demands a greater supply of water for use in industries and households. In fact, at home the average person uses **4500 litres** of water a year! We should be ashamed of such waste, as water is a very precious commodity.

SAVE WATER

Please turn OFF the tap after use.

Do you waste water at home?

How do you use water at home? Look at these facts and think about how you are contributing to wasting water:

- It takes **9 litres** of water to flush the toilet each time.
- A dishwasher (on average) uses **40 litres** of water each time it runs.
- Having a bath uses about **80 litres** of water.
- A running tap uses over **6 litres** of water per minute.

What can you do?

Think about putting a brick in the cistern of your toilet which will take up space so that there is less water to flush each time. How about washing up instead of using the dishwasher? A shower uses only **20 litres** of water – why not shower rather than bathe? How often do you leave the tap running when you are brushing your teeth, washing vegetables or washing your hands? Why not turn it off while you are brushing your teeth, wash your vegetables in a bowl and half fill the sink with water to wash your hands?

These are only a very few tips that would help to save water – there are many more. Why not do some research yourself about how water is wasted, so that you can be **WATER-FRIENDLY**? We need to think about it today; tomorrow is not good enough if we really value our natural resources.

Language and meaning

Practice activities

1. A rhetorical question is a question that the reader is not expected to answer. Write down one example of this from the text. What effect is it meant to have on the reader?

_____

_____

_____

2. Write down the sentence that uses very emotive language in the first paragraph.

_____

_____

Test-style questions

1. How many litres of water are used during a shower? Circle **one** answer.

    20   **80**   **40**   **6**   *1 mark*

2. How could you save water when washing vegetables?

_____

1 mark

3. How could you save water when cleaning your teeth?

_____

1 mark

4. Why do we need to save water?

_____

_____

1 mark

Evidence from the text

Key to comprehension

It is important that you back up your answers with **evidence from the text**. Sometimes, you might use a direct quotation to do this.

For example, if you are commenting on a text about the health benefits of fruit, you might say:

The text tells us that oranges are full of vitamin C, so they are very healthy.

Alternatively, you could express the same information using a direct quotation:

The text says "oranges contain a lot of vitamin C", so they are very healthy.

Top tip

Look out for key details in between the "selling points" when reading a leaflet.

Comprehension material

Treetops Fun

Join us at Treetops Fun for a unique, exciting and fun-packed experience. Our awesome High Ropes Course contains over 80 exciting obstacles. Different heights and different challenges for different abilities make it the perfect day out for the whole family! Amaze yourself as you tackle the challenges head on, from mid-air jumps to speedy zips. You'll swing through them all!

You do not need to be a climber or an abseiler. You don't need to be superman. Absolutely NO experience or skill is required for this activity, just a willingness to have a great adventure! The instructors train you, connect you to the course and then you are off!

Everyone aged 6+ can come and enjoy the fun! Children can do the course on their own with parents watching.

Birthday Fun!

How about having the most awesome birthday party ever? Book a treetop adventure for you and your friends. We cater for parties of adults and children. Please telephone for further details.

Booking

You can book online or by telephone (number and website address on back of leaflet).

Opening times

We are open all year round (except Christmas Day) between 9am and 5pm. Why not give it a go and conquer some of the biggest, most fun challenges of your life?

Evidence from the text

Practice activities

1. Can the whole family go on the course? Explain your answer using direct quotations from the text.

   _____

   _____

   _____

   _____

2. How can you book your adventure?

   a) _____   b) _____

Test-style questions

1. Identify an adjective used in the first sentence and describe its effect on the reader.

   _____

   _____

   2 marks

2. What two challenges are mentioned in the first paragraph?

   _____   _____   *2 marks*

3. In your own words, explain what the leaflet is advertising.

   _____

   1 mark

4. Would you want to go with your whole family? Explain your reasons clearly, using evidence from the leaflet.

   _____

   _____

   2 marks

Justifying opinions

Key to comprehension

When reading non-fiction texts, particularly discussion texts, you are faced with different opinions about issues. It is up to you as the reader to decide what you believe, but you need to be able to justify your opinions.

This could mean using arguments made in the text to support your opinion, or it could mean using your own arguments (which the author may not have considered).

Comprehension material

Should mobile phones be allowed in schools?

There has been a huge increase in the number of new communication technologies available in the last few years. This, of course, includes mobile phones. In fact, it is estimated that over 80% of young people aged 10–14 now own their own phone. Following a number of instances of phones being used inappropriately in schools, there has been a great deal of debate in the press as to whether pupils should be allowed to take their mobile phones into school.

There are undeniably positive benefits in children being able to communicate freely. Parents like to know that their child is safe and can contact them if necessary, and mobile phones cater to this. Because of them, parents feel they can give their children more independence, allowing their children, for instance, to travel to and from school on their own, which can have its own hazards.

Schools, on the other hand, argue that a child carrying a mobile phone could make them more vulnerable to being mugged, both on the journeys to and from school and in the playground. This is backed up by police figures that show a high proportion of crimes committed against young people involve thefts of mobile phones. A further concern voiced by schools is that mobile phones can create a competitive atmosphere, making some children, who do not own the "best model" or perhaps do not own a phone at all, feel left out. The final (and possibly most important) argument against mobile phones, is that they are used in class and distract from learning.

The debate remains open and will continue to do so for the foreseeable future. Meanwhile, it is up to individual schools to set the rules as they see fit, and parents / children to break them as they see fit!

Justifying opinions

Practice activities

1. Which side of the argument do you agree with and why?

    _____

    _____

2. Why is it likely the argument will continue to be debated in the future?

    _____

Test-style questions

1. Which of these are arguments **for** allowing phones in schools?

    Tick **two**

    Parents can contact their children. ☐

    Children can communicate freely. ☐

    Children are more likely to be mugged. ☐

    Mobile phones distract from learning. ☐   *1 mark*

2. Write another argument to add to the paragraph about why phones should be allowed in schools, thinking carefully about another use for them.

    _____

    _____

    1 mark

3. What does the author imply in the words: "and parents / children to break them as they see fit" and how does this relate to the phone issue?

    _____

    _____

    2 marks

Summarising ideas

Being able to **summarise** the ideas in a text is an important skill, especially when a text is very long and contains a lot of information. If you can summarise the information, it will mean you can remember the key points more easily and make use of them. For example:

- If you have a long list of instructions, you might summarise them into a short to-do list.
- If you are going on holiday, you might read through a travel guide and summarise which attractions are really worth seeing, or the phrases that will be really useful.

Comprehension material

Planning Department
County Hall
Mudgeley MT4 8QT

15 Bart Terrace
Mudgeley MT8 4BE

20th December

Dear Mr Grieves,

We are writing in response to the plans you submitted to our offices on 15th November this year regarding your proposed extension. Firstly, we apologise for the delay in writing but the address that you sent the letter to was in fact our Education Department, rather than our Planning Department. The plans that you sent were difficult to read due to their handwritten nature, and we also had to take advice from our county architects.

However, we are now able to offer you a response to your letter. We deem it necessary for you to clarify the drawings that are in support of your proposal in order that we can finalise details, but in essence we are in favour of your proposal. From our records, there is no reason to think that your plans will interfere with any public or private access, and you therefore do not need to seek further advice from the Highways Agency.

To proceed, we require that you provide us with the architect's plans for your proposed extension **within 14 days**. These plans will then be checked before we are able to come to a final decision and possibly issue a ticket of certification.

Please send your plans marked for the attention of **The Planning Department**.

Yours sincerely,

P Lanning

Summarising ideas

Practice activities

1. Summarise why the Planning Department's response was delayed.

_____

_____

2. Summarise what needs to happen next.

_____

_____

Test-style questions

1. Who is the author of the original letter? Circle **one** answer.

Mr Hall   **P Lanning**   **Mr Grieves**   **Mudgeley**   _1 mark_

2. What is meant by the word "proceed" in the third paragraph?

Tick **one**

prevent ☐

continue ☐

start ☐

help ☐   _1 mark_

3. Has the Planning Department definitely agreed to the extension? Explain your answer fully using evidence from the text.

_____

_____

_____

2 marks

71

Acknowledgements

The author and publisher are grateful to the copyright holders for permission to use quoted materials and images.

P10 from *Grandpa Chatterji*, copyright © 1993 Jamila Gavin; first published in Great Britain 1993 by Methuen Children's Books Limited, reproduced with kind permission of David Higham Associates Ltd; P12 from *Balaclava Boy* by Richard Parkyn, reproduced with the kind permission of Richard Parkyn; P14 from *The Case of the Missing Stamp* from 20 MINI MYSTERIES by Dina Anastasio, originally published by Scholastic Children's Books 1989, copyright © Dina Anastasio; P22 from *Journey to Jo'berg* by Beverley Naidoo; reproduced by permission of The Agency (London) Ltd © 1985 Beverley Naidoo, all rights reserved and enquiries to The Agency (London) Ltd, 24 Pottery Lane, London W11 4LZ; P26 from *Collins Big Cat: Tig in the Dumps* by Michaela Morgan, published by HarperCollins Publishers; P54 "Farr's Field Letter", P62 "Tabs Comes Home" reproduced with the kind permission of Alison Head.

All images are © Shutterstock.com, ©Jupiterimages, or ©Letts Educational, an imprint of HarperCollins*Publishers*.

All facts are correct at time of going to press.

Published by Letts Educational
An imprint of HarperCollins*Publishers*
77–85 Fulham Palace Road
London W6 8JB

ISBN 9781844197446

First published 2013

01/101013

10 9 8 7 6 5 4 3 2 1

British Library Cataloguing in Publication Data.

A CIP record of this book is available from the British Library.

Commissioning Editor: Tammy Poggo
Author: Rachel Axten-Higgs
Project Editor: Daniel Dyer
Cover Design: Paul Oates
Inside Concept Design: Ian Wrigley
Layout: Jouve India Private Limited
Production: Robert Smith
Printed in China

MIX
Paper from
responsible sources
FSC
www.fsc.org   FSC™ C007454